Finding Unexpected Gifts in Unexpected Places

KARYN MONTGOMERY

WESTBOW
PRESS
A DIVISION OF THOMAS NELSON
& ZONDERVAN

Copyright © 2014 Karyn Montgomery.

All rights reserved. No part of this book may be used or reproduced by any means, graphic, electronic, or mechanical, including photocopying, recording, taping or by any information storage retrieval system without the written permission of the publisher except in the case of brief quotations embodied in critical articles and reviews.

Scripture taken from the Holy Bible, NEW INTERNATIONAL VERSION®. Copyright © 1973, 1978, 1984 by Biblica, Inc. All rights reserved worldwide. Used by permission. NEW INTERNATIONAL VERSION® and NIV® are registered trademarks of Biblica, Inc. Use of either trademark for the offering of goods or services requires the prior written consent of Biblica US, Inc.

WestBow Press books may be ordered through booksellers or by contacting:

WestBow Press
A Division of Thomas Nelson & Zondervan
1663 Liberty Drive
Bloomington, IN 47403
www.westbowpress.com
1 (866) 928-1240

Because of the dynamic nature of the Internet, any web addresses or links contained in this book may have changed since publication and may no longer be valid. The views expressed in this work are solely those of the author and do not necessarily reflect the views of the publisher, and the publisher hereby disclaims any responsibility for them.

Any people depicted in stock imagery provided by Thinkstock are models, and such images are being used for illustrative purposes only. Certain stock imagery © Thinkstock.

ISBN: 978-1-4908-5352-9 (sc)
ISBN: 978-1-4908-5353-6 (hc)
ISBN: 978-1-4908-5354-3 (e)

Library of Congress Control Number: 2014917333

Printed in the United States of America.

WestBow Press rev. date: 10/03/2014

Contents

Introduction vii

My Grandfather, My Mom, and Me

My Grandfather 1

My Mom 3

Me 11

Unexpected Gifts

The Gift of Identity 33

The Gift of Kindness 39

The Gift of Compassion 47

The Gift of Wholehearted Trust 53

The Gift of Gratitude 61

The Gift of Grace 67

The Gift of Friendship 73

The Gift of Life through Death 79

The Gift of Giving 89

Marked by His Presence 97

Introduction

This is a story of God's goodness and of discovering gifts in life's challenges. God reveals Himself in many ways through both the joys of life and the pains. Some of the most profound and transformative gifts that I have received have come through the tough experiences. They have drawn me into a closer relationship with my Lord and Savior, Jesus Christ.

In this series of reflections, I have focused on the unexpected gifts that have transformed my life. In doing this, I have traced a short bit of my family history. This story spans three generations, and my story is most deeply connected to my mother's.

Each of us has a story to tell. Mine is at once common and uncommon, ordinary and extraordinary, as is yours. These stories contain the unique details of our lives through which God reveals Himself and through which we can find Him.

You may see glimpses of yourself in my story. If so, I pray that you will find encouragement and inspiration and that your life will be transformed into one marked by God's presence and clothed in His grace.

Look deeper.

My Grandfather, My Mom, and Me

My Grandfather

I don't know much about him. What I do know I learned from my mother. William Terry was a quiet and kind man. The father of eight children, he lost his beloved wife, Alvina, following the birth of twins. His fourth child, Barbara, my mother, was just five when her beloved Mama died. Barbara and her father had loved her dearly, this beautiful woman of Swedish descent, and their lives would never be the same after losing her.

This tragedy marked William with a sadness that stayed with him for the rest of his life like a cloud that never dissipated. He was at times lonely, and as a child, Barbara often heard him say with tears in his eyes, "Oh, if only Mama had lived." And she often heard him singing "In the Garden." It would become one of Barbara's favorite hymns.

I come to the garden alone

While the dew is still on the roses

And the voice I hear falling on my ear

The Son of God discloses.

And He walks with me, and He talks with me,

And He tells me I am His own;

And the joy we share as we tarry there

None other has ever known.

My Mom

On a bitterly cold day in Superior, Wisconsin, during the winter of 1932, Barbara's daddy took her to kindergarten, walking with her onto the playground. Barbara was proud of her handsome father, a tall, olive-skinned man with curly hair. Her daddy was the manager of the Chevrolet dealership in town and always wore a suit and tie to work. Barbara was proud to be seen with him until that sad day at school when another child asked, "Is your daddy a [n-word]?"

    How could anyone say such a thing about her beloved daddy? It was a knife in the heart of this sensitive child, who was still grieving the loss of her mother. Her soul was seared. She had no idea why someone would ask this question. After all, she thought of this man simply as her beloved daddy. Perhaps it was the curious tone of the child's voice. Perhaps it was the scornful look on the child's face. Somehow Barbara knew that this child had used a very bad word to ask a question about her daddy.

Several years later, Barbara's father married the housekeeper, Miss Finnegan, who had been with the family since Alvina died. Miss Finnegan loved the twins like they were her own. This wasn't surprising since she had mothered them from birth. The other six children knew these were the favored kids.

Miss Finnegan seemed to dislike Barbara. She punished her harshly, repeatedly making her sit in a dark closet for what seemed like hours on end as punishment for some childish misdeed. During these long hours in the closet, Barbara became a survivor. She developed a will of steel and grew determined someday to gain the respect of others. She dreamed of a college education. She dreamed of having her own children and being the mother to them that she did not have herself.

Barbara also dreamed of a lovely home with fine furnishings and of having a gracious and refined life. But when her father went away to work in Greenland during World War II, Barbara found herself homeless. Miss Finnegan had no use for her and sent her away from the family home. She was thirteen. How Barbara's father reacted to Miss Finnegan's actions when he finally returned is one of many unanswered questions.

Left to her own resources, Barbara ran an ad in the local paper offering to work for room and board. A prominent pharmacist in town hired her as the household help and gave her a place to live. She worked diligently for the family, envied the children who had both a mother and a father, and marveled at their fine lifestyle.

As Thanksgiving approached that year, Barbara looked forward to an extravagant meal seated with the family in the lovely formal dining room. When the holiday arrived, she found the family and guests seated and served, but she was told to serve herself and retire to the upstairs bedroom to eat her Thanksgiving dinner alone. Barbara could not understand such rejection. She was baffled and hurt. Not long after, the family asked her to leave, though no one gave her a reason. Barbara was once again left to her own resources.

Miss Johansen, a kind physical education teacher at the local junior high school, offered Barbara a temporary place to live. She was a gracious Christian lady who epitomized refined taste and proper etiquette. Her example fueled Barbara's desire for gracious living and the respect that came with it.

In and out of the family home, Barbara was especially close to her brother Don, who was just ahead of her in the line-up of eight siblings. He would look out for her whenever he could.

One day Barbara went to the movies with a friend. In stern Miss Finnegan's mind, this was considered a mortal sin. On her way back to the family home, Barbara found a note that Don had scrawled in chalk on the pavement. He wrote, "Barb, don't lie. Miss Finnegan knows you went to the movies." Don's loving brotherly protection helped Barbara to fear Miss Finnegan just a little bit less.

Soon after, Don enlisted in the US Navy as a radioman and sadly was a crew member on a plane shot down by the enemy over the Pacific Ocean during World War II. Once again Barbara's heart was broken, and she never got over his loss. She would weep each time she spoke of him, even decades later.

By the time Barbara was sixteen, her two older sisters, now young adults, were living in Chicago. They took her in and Barbara stayed with them for a short while, working at Billings Hospital to earn her keep. She put in long hours, unprotected, in the tuberculosis ward. There she gained her love of nursing, caring for people who were sick and in need.

The Korean War was under way when Barbara graduated from high school, and she enlisted, becoming among the first women to gain permanent status in the US Navy. It was in the service that Barbara met the love of her life, K. James Risley. Jim was a happy-go-lucky fellow, full of good humor and loads of fun to be with. Given his extraordinary good nature, Barbara felt certain that he must have come from a happy family.

Barbara and Jim served in the Navy Dental Corps as dental assistants. Jim's brother, Jerry, served in the same unit. As Barbara and Jim's relationship began to blossom, Jerry reported home to his mother that Barbara "looked like an Indian." Yes, Barbara had the same beautiful olive complexion that her dad had, but that was of no consequence to Jim. He saw only the love of his life—a sensitive, gracious, beautiful, refined young woman.

After a five-month courtship, Barbara and Jim were married on Christmas Day 1949, much to the dismay of Jim's parents. The wedding was small, attended only by Jim's family and Barbara's younger brother, John. Barbara never understood why Jim's parents did not accept her. They were rude and dismissive, critical and demeaning toward a young bride already insecure after enduring life's uncertainties and cruelties. She did her best to undo their dislike, but to no avail. Did they think she was not white enough?

Shortly after their marriage, Jim was deployed to Korea, serving on a hospital ship for two years. Barbara remained at her duty station in San Francisco, California, and eagerly awaited

Jim's return. Their love only grew stronger during their long separation as newlyweds. While away, Jim purchased a beautiful pearl ring and sent it to his bride for her twenty-fourth birthday. He penned a note, which he enclosed with the ring:

>To my darling wife
>on her 24th birthday.
>To you my love, whom I adore,
>and will be my love forevermore!
>
>Happy birthday, my darling—
>would that I could be with you this day.
>I'd love you just constantly.
>May you never be without me
>on this your day—ever again.
>
>The large pearl for my love—
>as endless as the depth of a pearl, so is my love for you.
>
>The first black pearl for my
>devotion to you—
>as full and rich as the

wondrous beauty of this stone,
so is my devotion to you.

The second black pearl for my
adoration and trueness to you.
The most perfect of perfection in this black pearl is
merely a minute fraction of the true perfection of my
admiration and adoration of you.
The perfectness the pearl tries to obtain can never be
compared to the faithfulness and trueness with which
I belong to you.

Happy birthday, my beloved—my wife. I'll always love you.

Yours,

Jim

Jim was a man of strong character and unflinching commitment who stood loyally by his young bride. His parents' refusal to accept her eventually resulted in complete estrangement. Not even through marriage was Barbara to acquire the mother she so desperately longed to have and missed her entire life after losing her own.

When they completed their military service, Barbara and Jim settled in California, and Jim enrolled in the University of California at Riverside. During this time their first two daughters were born. I was the second. I was six weeks old when my father graduated from college. He became the first in his family to earn a college degree.

Following his graduation in June of 1956, my father went to work for the Firestone Tire and Rubber Company in Southgate, California. Over the next few years, the family grew to include a son and another daughter. Mom was the dutiful and devoted wife, while Dad worked diligently to climb the corporate ladder. Our young family moved from Huntington Beach to Pomona to Garden Grove, California, to better accommodate Dad's long work hours and commute.

Me

I was a playful child with good friends even before the age of five. To this day I remember my friend Petra's death following a brief illness. I didn't understand how someone could pass away so suddenly. Her death caused me to become a kind and sensitive child who valued family members and playmates. When I was in kindergarten and first grade, my teachers told my mother that I was the most well-liked child in the class. I was a happy-go-lucky, carefree girl skipping through childhood.

In 1962, Dad was promoted and transferred to a newly built Firestone plant in Salinas, California, where he became the manager for methods and standards. Our family was proud of Dad's promotion. My mother was especially glad to see her husband's career taking off. In the early 1960s, a woman's status depended greatly on her husband's position.

Mom and Dad moved their family to Salinas, built a home in a desirable neighborhood, and sent their kids off to a respected elementary school right around the corner. Mom acquired lovely and gracious furnishings, sterling silver, crystal, and a parlor grand piano. She was beginning to realize her childhood dreams. She loved to entertain, often hosting dinner parties for church friends and for Dad's executive colleagues. At the same time, she volunteered at the Victory Mission, a shelter on skid row. She never forgot what it was like to be in need.

While my mother gained a sense of status through my father's advancements, she never lost her thirst for her own development. As our family settled into a normal middle-class routine, Mom enrolled in San Jose State University, commuting sixty miles each way to classes three days a week and eventually earning a bachelor's degree in sociology. She became the first and only one of her siblings to earn a college degree. Still she dreamed of nursing. My mother was my inspiration, a living lesson about the importance of education.

Those early elementary school years changed my life forever. Arriving as a new kid in the second grade at Monterey Park Elementary School, I was greeted by two viciously mean seven-year-old boys, Craig Meekly and Jim Wills. (I have changed their last names.) They made fun of me mercilessly, calling me "fat lips," "[n-word] lips," "big eyes," "monkey knees," and "ugly." Craig Meekly's unkindness toward me was unrelenting. This was an experience I had never encountered before. I was dumbfounded.

I tried to ignore these two boys and to act like they didn't hurt my feelings. But sadly, I began to believe them. Once self-confident, winsome, and playful, I became self-conscious, shy, and ashamed, imprisoned in my own body by the wounds that had penetrated my soul. To this day I abhor the word *ugly*. My favorite childhood story was "The Ugly Duckling." I could relate to the "ugly" chick and hoped and prayed that I too would someday become beautiful like the swan.

When I had finished seventh grade, Dad was once again transferred—this time across the country to Quincy, Illinois. To a girl born and raised in California, Illinois seemed a strange and foreign land. Quincy was an old, still somewhat segregated Mississippi River town, with brick streets leading to a massive junior high school. I walked there with my siblings. The weather was beastly hot and humid in the summer and fall of my first year there. I missed the ocean and found the muddy waters of the Mississippi to be a bleak consolation.

I was timid and self-conscious. How would I be received? Someone suggested that my California tan made me "look like an Indian," but that was the only comment about my appearance that I recall. I managed to make friends, but not any close ones. My friends were the pretty girls, the popular girls, but I certainly did not consider myself one of them.

Determined to find a place for myself and to gain the respect of my peers, I immersed myself in my schoolwork. Soon I was earning all As. When I completed my freshman year of high school with straight As, I found my personal challenge. I set out to graduate with nothing but As. By doing this, I felt I would prove myself worthy of acceptance by my peers.

I began to be noticed by boys again, this time not in demeaning and unkind ways, but in affirming ways for the very qualities I valued about myself. I had a few nominal boyfriends, and during my junior year, one young man took a particular interest in me. He was a nice guy, a kind guy, one year older. He was popular and his friends were among the "in" crowd. He was from a prominent family in town. This young man asked me for a date. He thought I was pretty even though I did not believe him. He accepted me as I was. The young man was Bob Montgomery, and I would marry him five years later.

Look Deeper

The summer before my senior year, I got a letter from a prominent Quincy resident, saying that I had been recommended to compete in the Miss Teenage Quincy Pageant. Me, the ugly girl with big eyes and fat lips? How could that be? Maybe I was not as ugly as I thought. Although I couldn't see it, I was told my eyes were beautiful. I had prayed that I would "grow into" my lips. Maybe my prayer had been answered. Surely they weren't "n-word lips." But when I looked in the mirror, I still saw an ugly girl with big eyes and fat lips.

With my mother's encouragement, I entered the contest, and much to my surprise, I won. It must have been because the judges wanted someone "smart," I told myself. Hiding my timidity and lack of self-confidence, I waved from the backs of convertibles in local parades and went on to compete in the Miss Teenage America Pageant in Fort Worth, Texas, in the fall of 1973. I did not win, but I believe that I impressed the judges with a flawless piano rendition of Beethoven's Pathetique Sonata as my talent performance.

Later that year, I was voted by my high school peers to be a member of the annual May dance court, an honor usually going to the cute and popular girls. Maybe I was indeed cute and popular in the eyes of my peers; maybe I had indeed been transformed from the ugly duckling to the lovely swan. But in my eyes, I was still that girl who in second grade had been told she was ugly, with big eyes and fat lips.

I graduated from high school in June of 1974 as valedictorian, one of four students with perfect academic records in a class of more than five hundred students. I had achieved my goal, earning the respect of my peers. Miss Teenage Quincy, May dance attendant, class valedictorian. I looked at my photos, trying to see an attractive girl but seeing only an impostor. I discounted the compliments of others. Those viciously mean boys in second grade had stolen my self-esteem many years before.

"N-word lips." Why did the words wound my soul so deeply? Yes, I had full lips at a time when pencil-thin lips were fashionable. My two sisters had pencil-thin lips, and I didn't understand how mine could be so opposite. I learned to use lip liner on the inside edges in an attempt to minimize their appearance. I had been ridiculed for the fullness of my lips as if there were something wrong with them, and that left an open wound in my heart. Beyond that, my lips had been associated in a cruel and demeaning way with "Negro" attributes at a time when those features were not viewed as desirable.

After graduating from high school, I began studies at the college I had dreamed of attending, Wheaton College, in Wheaton, Illinois. Here I was among many high school valedictorians, and I worked extremely hard to graduate with high honors. I had a few close friends and many casual ones.

My relationship with my high school sweetheart continued and grew stronger even though we attended different colleges. Bob was in Iowa. He would call home for money and then, unbeknownst to his parents, drive six hours each way to and from Wheaton on the weekends so that we could spend a few short hours together. We missed each other when we were apart. In his junior year, Bob transferred to Elmhurst College, just a few minutes from Wheaton. I'm sure his parents were glad too, as the requests for deposits to his checking account became less frequent!

In August of 1977, I married the kindest man I had ever known. Bob has been my beloved husband for thirty-seven years and counting. During the first nine years of our marriage, my husband became established in his work and I also enjoyed a fulfilling career. I considered various professional or graduate academic pursuits, but we knew that when we had a family, one of us would be the at-home parent. We both wanted that parent to be me, so I chose to defer further study toward a professional career.

Just before our ninth wedding anniversary, our first son was born. David was a beautiful baby, often attracting attention from admirers. One of them commented on his beautiful olive skin, and I proudly attributed that to my mother's genes. When I gazed at my baby boy, I resolved that no matter what else he became in life, he would be kind and compassionate. I would teach David never to be unkind, never to bully or to call names, and never to demean someone's appearance, especially a girl's.

Two years later our second son was born—another beautiful boy, this one with curly hair. *Where in the world did that come from?* I wondered. His dad had wavy hair, and there was curly hair on both sides of our family, so the answer seemed clear. Everyone loved Michael's curls, and as a child he never disliked them, to my knowledge. Once again, I was determined that this boy, like his older brother, would be kind and compassionate. He would be taught never to demean someone else, especially a girl.

During our sons' elementary school years, my mother shared a curious recent finding with me. She was nervous when she did so. On all the birth certificates of the eight siblings in her family, both mother and father were listed as "white"—except on one. Much to the dismay of all, one sister's birth certificate stated that her father was "colored." Dismissed as the incorrect assumption of the recording clerk, who had probably noted her father's curly hair and olive-colored skin, the designation was completely discounted. What did it matter anyway? The eight siblings and their offspring were all clearly white.

Nonetheless, my mother was disturbed, having revisited a sensitive subject first raised on that dreadful day when, as a five-year-old child, she had been asked, "Is your daddy a [n-word]?" She told me that she had never wanted to display a picture of her mother and father in our family home, for fear that I or one of my siblings might ask the same question that had hurt her so deeply as a child.

The subject continued to stir curiosity among my mother's siblings and some of their children. Although the family tree was difficult to trace with certainty, my mother's brother informed her one day that indeed there was a possibility that they "had some dark blood" in them. She remained dismissive, citing all the reasons to the contrary, and the question was swept under the rug.

But it was not to stay there. Soon family members began to discuss the question more openly. Some accepted the possibility of mixed-race ancestry as likely truth, believing that my mother's father, my grandfather, may have been half black and half white. As word reached my sons through their curious cousins, they received the news as amusing, a sort of badge of honor. While we as a culture still have a long way to go, they live in a much more integrated world where diversity is valued. And they had learned not to judge others by the color of their skin. They began to suggest that their great-grandfather may have been biracial.

During his college years, my elder son worked at a group home for troubled teen boys. One of the black boys joked that my son had "n-word lips." Did it bother my son? Not in the least. He knew this was not said to demean. He knew that he had beautifully sculpted lips, the kind that girls would die to kiss and the kind that people these days pay big bucks to get!

My second son's curly hair is his signature, admired and envied by his peers. They see it as very cool, his unique characteristic. When he was working in Uganda one summer while in college, his curly hair made him an instant celebrity among the African children. After all, he had white skin and their hair! Very cool indeed.

When I began to hear family jokes and insinuations about our possible heritage, I was troubled, afraid that my sons would at some point feel the same sting that my mother and I had felt all those years before. What if they were rejected on that basis by the women they would someday fall in love with? I am ashamed for this fear. My dear sons assured me that my concerns were not the mind-set of their generation. They were proud of their heritage, whether or not it included "dark blood." They thought it made their story more interesting. They confronted me one day in front of their peers, and their loving nudges and jokes about my grandfather, their great-grandfather, helped me begin to accept who I am and who I may be.

I also feared facing myself. What if it was true? What if my lips belied my identity all along? What if those two cruel boys in second grade had been right? What does it matter anyway? It matters in that my story may be a common one, unbeknownst to others like me. And there are many lessons to be gleaned from that likely reality. It matters in that we must never be judged by the color of our skin—white, black, or brown. The truth may lie hidden in our genes.

My two sons and their beautiful and accepting wives have unknowingly bandaged the wounds in my heart inflicted a half-century ago. They are my pride and joy. My sons were unusually kind boys who grew up to become compassionate, sensitive, empathetic, accepting young men, like their father. To my knowledge, neither has ever bullied anyone, especially a girl, or demeaned a girl's appearance. In fact, they are active in seeking out and extending kindnesses to those on the fringes. They have a high respect for women, and even at times forgo their white male privilege for the benefit of others less privileged. They are strikingly handsome young men, one with decidedly curly hair, both with sculpted, gorgeous, full lips. One has the fair skin of his father and his Swedish and English ancestors, and the other has skin that tans easily, like mine and his grandmother's.

I don't know if my mother ever embraced the possibility that her father may have been biracial. We never discussed it apart from what has been related here. My mother was an empathetic, sensitive person, always giving and caring about others in need. Because of the pain in her childhood, she was a sensitive person, easily hurt by the thoughtlessness or perceived slights and rejections of others. But she was a resilient survivor, greeting each day with the joy of the Lord in her heart. Not having a mother of her own growing up, she wanted nothing more in life than to be a good mother to her own children, the mother she did not have and whom she missed her entire life. And indeed she was. She taught me to value the important role and high calling of being a wife and a mother.

In her final years, my mother found her greatest joy and satisfaction. The last eight years of my father's life were spent in the middle to advanced stages of Alzheimer's disease, complicated by the effects of a massive stroke. Mom and Dad had finally completed my mother's dream home, a lovely, modest two-story house that resembled her childhood home. My mother's brother came to visit, and they recalled a day long ago in their childhood when they had been sent out from the family home without dinner for misbehaving. Walking together, they gazed at a lovely home in the distance, and my mother told her brother that someday she would have a home like that one. She indeed achieved her childhood dream.

During those final years, my mother cared for her beloved husband of more than fifty years with the greatest devotion, diligence, selflessness, and love imaginable. A renewed love story unfolded before my eyes. Living in the same town, I watched as my mother gave my completely disabled father the finest care possible. He could not walk. He could not talk. He could not feed himself. He could not comprehend. He did not know his family. He could do nothing for himself. He was completely dependent on others, just like an infant. My mother never tired of the nonstop demands of caring for a complete invalid, from providing bed baths and diaper changes to doing endless laundry to meeting medical needs to preparing nutritious meals. Even when my father's swallowing became compromised, my mother would lovingly cook and puree all his foods.

My mother offered this care for a full five years, the last years of her life. She had indeed become a fine nurse and achieved her final dream. And she wished her in-laws could have known what a devoted and good wife she had been to their son.

During these last five years my mother's health began to fail. She was diagnosed with kidney cancer in the late summer of 2005. The affected kidney was removed, and we thought all was well. She went on with her life as if it was, but in the fall of 2007 the cancer returned—this time on her spine. The prognosis was grim, eleven months to live on average, but my mother remained hopeful. Her primary concern continued to be my father's care, and she hoped to outlive him since he was so dependent upon her.

For Christmas of 2007, my brother and his wife along with my family took my mother on a cruise to the Bahamas. We had a beautiful last Christmas together, one that we will always cherish. My brother sang "White Christmas" to my mother before a large audience in honor of her marriage to our father that Christmas Day fifty-eight years past.

My mother and father had always enjoyed dancing together, and when my father lost his ability to walk, dancing with him was the pleasure my mother missed the most. On this cruise, she danced at every opportunity. My college-student sons danced proudly with their frail, terminally ill grandmother. She seemed to be young again.

For a Moment

There she sat
On the steps of the grand ballroom,
Listening to the music of a live dance band.
The music was her partner
And transported her in memory
To happy times,
Dancing times with her beloved,
Long-ago times.

With eager anticipation, she asked,
"Sons, will you dance with me?"
With timid feet they agreed,
Sons for their father;
And once again she was transported to happy times,
Dancing times with her beloved,
Long-ago times.

Her weak body, fragile, and breathless,

With glowing eyes and brilliant smile,

Dancing, dancing, dancing,

Remembering happy times,

Dancing times with her beloved,

Long-ago times.

"Grandsons, will you dance with me?"

So they danced,

Grandsons for their grandpa;

Dancing, dancing, dancing, like the first time,

Remembering happy times,

Dancing times with her beloved,

Long-ago times.

For brief moments

No more cancer, no more Alzheimer's, no more stroke,

Remembering happy times,

Dancing times with her beloved,

Long-ago times.

She danced

Like no one was watching,

Remembering happy times.

Dancing times with her beloved,

Long-ago times.

It was the best of times.

Just ten months later, on October 9, 2008, ravaged by the toxic effects of chemotherapy and radiation treatments, my beloved mother passed away at my father's bedside. On one of the days preceeding her death, my father uttered the words, "Barbara, love forever." He had not spoken in years. Little did we know that my dear father was hanging on to life for her sake. He passed away just seven days later, on October 16, 2008. They had been married two months short of fifty-nine years.

It has been six blurry years since we came to the garden "while the dew was still on the roses" and buried my mother and father following a joint memorial service honoring their life together. As my mother and father were welcomed to their eternal home, we tarried there in the garden and were comforted knowing that we are God's own—all of us. We belong to Him.

Experiencing life with my mother and father during their final years, contending at the same time with advanced Alzheimer's disease and terminal cancer, and walking them the same week to their eternal home were at once the most traumatic and transformative experiences of my life. I felt grief so deep that at times I wished I had been the one who had died.

Those years were a long, lonely, and difficult passage, but one filled with profound lessons for living, as are the other experiences that I have shared in this reflection. The hardships, pain, and heartbreaks that my mother and I shared are sources of strength that continue to transform my life. And that is the reason I am sharing this story. Although in many ways ordinary experiences, there are extraordinary lessons for living to be gleaned from them, lessons for living life to the fullest—ultimately, unexpected gifts.

Unexpected Gifts

The Gift of Identity

"And He walks with me, and He talks with me, and He tells me I am His own." Oh, the power in those words of my grandfather's favorite hymn, "In the Garden."

The setting of this well-loved hymn is a beautiful garden in the early morning, the dew still sparkling on the roses. A solitary guest drops by to visit. The sweet voice the visitor hears is the voice of the Lord. God walks with him. God talks with him and tells him that he belongs to the Father in heaven. The joy shared by the garden visitor and God is like none ever known.

The songwriter may have used the garden with its roses as a metaphor for life. In life there is great beauty, symbolized by the roses. Life is delicate, as is the rose. But just as roses have thorns, so the beauty of life comes with its share of pain. We know that this lone visitor arrives in the morning, given the presence of dew.

From what little I know of my grandfather, I can only assume that this was his favorite hymn because he related to the experience of that solitary garden visitor. Perhaps my grandfather was a lonely man. My mother often recalled a certain sadness about him. Perhaps he felt that he never belonged, but in those garden moments with God, found joy like none other, the joy of belonging.

What I can only assume to be true of my grandfather I know to be true of my mother. In her early adult years, she was "pitifully shy," as she would tell us. But she overcame her shyness, her self-consciousness, and found her place when she found her belonging, her identity, in her faith in Christ. Then her life blossomed like the beautiful garden rose.

So where do we find our authentic identity, our objective, our distinguishing reality? Is it in how we are perceived or defined by others? Is it in our work? Is it in our associations? Is it in the color of our skin? Is it in our sexual orientation? The answer to this question is not about who we are but whose we are.

In 1 John 3.1, we read, "How great is the love the Father has lavished on us, that we should be called children of God. And that is what we are!" We are children of God! Did you get that? You are a child of the Creator of the universe, who cares deeply about you, loves you with an everlasting love, and has a plan and a purpose for your life! And the word *lavished* means poured out generously, abundantly, more than you can ask or imagine and more than you need.

Just as God's grace is lavished upon you, so is His great love for you. He has claimed you as His beloved. God, your heavenly Father, loves you, His child, beyond your ability to comprehend. And therein lies your true identity. Embrace this gift wholeheartedly. Believe it with all your heart and mind. When you do, nothing can separate you from the God who loves you so much that He gave His life that you might live. You have great value to Him—an identity as a child of God that transcends all others. This is the real you! Believe it and experience the joy that "none other has ever known."

"For you created my inmost being; you knit me together in my mother's womb. I praise you because I am fearfully and wonderfully made" (Ps. 139:13–14).

"How great is the love the Father has lavished on us, that we should be called children of God, and that is what we are!" (1 John 3:1).

"For we are God's workmanship, created in Christ Jesus to do good works, which God prepared in advance for us to do" (Eph. 2:10).

"I am convinced that neither death nor life, neither angels nor demons, neither the present nor the future, nor any powers, neither height nor depth, nor anything else in all creation, will be able to separate us from the love of God that is in Christ Jesus our Lord" (Rom. 8:38–39).

"For great is his love toward us, and the faithfulness of the Lord endures forever" (Ps. 117:2).

When we believe in Jesus Christ, we become children of God and have full access to our heavenly Father. We belong. We enjoy relational intimacy with God and are received into His family. God welcomes us into His house. The Creator of the universe delights in us!

Heavenly Father,

Your great love for me is incomprehensible. You have loved me with an everlasting love and have demonstrated Your love by giving Your life for me! Nothing can separate me from Your love. It is beyond my understanding to think that I am a child of the God of the universe and that You care deeply about me. You created me and I praise You. I believe Your Word, Lord, and thank You for Your great love for me.

I stand humbly in Your presence and claim Your love. I feel unworthy and tend to overlook my great value to You. Forgive me for minimizing Your love for me, Your child, and devaluing Your death for me when I fail to recognize my worth in Your eternal plan.

My identity is to be found in You alone and in Your awesome love for me. You have created me as Your child with a special combination of gifts that only I have been given. I am Your unique creation—Your child! I claim You as my heavenly Father and thank You for all that I can be through You.

Impress Your love upon me, Lord. Help me to know that who I am is not to be found in the stuff or the standards of this world. Keep me mindful that I belong to You and that You can use me in spite of my flaws and failures. Let me find my identity in You as Your child, with a special, God-given purpose for my life, and may I use my life for Your eternal purposes. Speak to me, Lord, and let me hear Your voice. May my spirit rest and be at peace in Your unfailing love for me.

In the name of my Father in heaven, I pray. Amen.

The Gift of Kindness

"Is your daddy a [n-word]?" "You have [n-word] lips." A question and a statement deeply wounded the hearts of two children. Bullying and racism are two topics at the forefront of our collective consciousness and of our national conversation. In my story and my mother's, the two are inextricably linked. For others, the issue may be one or the other. Both are destructive forces that cannot be minimized. And the consequences last for generations.

The consequences for me have been lifelong. The racist-tinged bullying to which I was subjected changed me as a child. This is the core reason bullying is cruel and wrong and must not be tolerated. It changes a child internally, and no person has the right to do such a dreadfully cruel thing to a child. The hurt caused by bullying cuts deep, and healing is sometimes a lifelong process.

At times when I see seven-year-old boys, I am amazed at how childish immaturity can so deeply damage another, as it did in my case and in my mother's. As an adult, I realize that I should be able to dismiss the cruelty I suffered, knowing that most kids who bully seek to tear down others because they don't like themselves. But the pain is never really forgotten. Damage done is damage done.

I bristle when I hear other adults dismiss the effects of bullying as insignificant. They claim that kids are resilient or that bullying is simply an inconvenient but inevitable part of growing up. No! It must not be tolerated, and we must do whatever is within our power to prevent it. We must diligently teach our kids that bullying is in the same category of wrongs as stealing. After all, it robs a person of self-esteem. We must teach our children to be kind. This is an urgent task for our society.

When I look at photos of myself as that sensitive, winsome seven-year- old girl, I feel like I'm having an out-of-body experience. The child I see is not ugly with "[n-word] lips" but is as cute as a button. And as a fifty-eight-year-old woman, I can look back now and see that those cruel boys were wrong, just as my mother tried to convince me at the time. An incredibly kind woman, my mother taught me the importance of kindness, primarily through this experience.

To this day, whenever I am tempted to make a less than complimentary comment about another, I remember a powerful lesson my mother taught me. She told me of a day when she was walking down the street with her father and muttered something unkind under her breath about a woman passing by. Her father told her, "Oh Barbara, don't say that. She may be somebody's mother." It was a lesson my mother never forgot. How well did she know the pain of a hurtful comment about somebody's loved one. I never knew my mother to speak an unkind word.

When I visited Atlanta, Georgia, for the first time recently, I was intrigued by the historical sites and exhibits connected with Martin Luther King Jr. The African Americans with whom I came in contact were unfailingly gracious, kind, polite, generous, and helpful as I toured the sites and visited the Ebenezer Baptist Church. I was conflicted by the mystery of my background as I admired these wonderful, strong, and resilient people. As a "white" visitor, I sensed no animosity. I was welcomed. I wanted to apologize for being part of the white community whose ancestors mistreated theirs. At the same time, in prideful moments, I dared to think that I might be one of them, that my great-grandfather may have been a slave. But I quickly dismissed such thoughts—my experience in life was in no way like theirs. I had been privileged because of my skin color, so I knew nothing that compared with their experience.

Kindness involves sympathetic, tenderhearted deeds and giving pleasure or relief to another. The many kindnesses I experienced while at the King historical sites and at the Ebenezer Baptist Church were profound and transformative. I was welcomed joyfully. I was embraced. I was offered a hand while singing a hymn. My African American brothers and sisters were a living testimony to the power of kindness. Their kindness to me was overwhelming. These brothers and sisters, a people who have experienced the worst cruelties, changed my heart forever. It was healed in part by their kindnesses to me, a stranger in their midst.

So I encourage you to practice random, deliberate acts of kindness. Everyone you meet has a story. Everyone has insecurities. Everyone has scars. No one gets through life unscathed. Be the balm of kindness. Live a life of kindness. How? You don't have to know another's story. You just have to respond in whatever tenderhearted way the circumstance demands. Kind words are life words. Choose your words to inspire. Remembering the kindness that you have experienced, pay it forward and give your own gift of kindness. You just may help to heal a hurting heart.

"You are kind and forgiving, O Lord, abounding in love to all who call to you" (Ps. 86:5).

"Love is patient, love is kind" (1 Cor. 13:4).

"Be kind and compassionate to one another" (Eph. 4:32).

"The Lord's servant… must be kind to everyone" (2 Tim. 2:24).

"Therefore, as God's chosen people, holy and dearly loved, clothe yourselves with compassion, kindness, humility, gentleness, and patience" (Col. 3:12).

"He was pierced for our transgressions, he was crushed for our iniquities; the punishment that brought us peace was upon him, and by his wounds we are healed" (Isa. 53:5).

Whatever harm others may have inflicted on you, let God use those experiences to soften your heart for His good. We all stand on the same ground at the foot of the cross. Claim God's overwhelming kindness and love for yourself. Hanging on to the truth of God's Word, let Jesus change your heart and your life so that you bring glory to Him through your kindness to others.

Kind and loving Father,

It's Your kindness that draws us to you.

I praise You, Lord, for You have created me with a unique purpose. All my life experiences contribute to that purpose.

I confess, Lord, that my thoughts and actions toward others are not always characterized by kindness, and I ask for Your forgiveness.

I want You to be Lord over my life.

I am grateful that Your plan for my life is perfect. Nothing is wasted.

Whatever hurts others have caused You can use for Your good. So I thank You for the pain. I give it to You and ask You to use me to point others to Your kindness.

Let my scars be scars of remembrance of Your great sacrifice for me. May I always be mindful that You were pierced for me and that through Your suffering we are healed.

Empower me to be kind, to be Your light of kindness. May my life be characterized by unfailing kindness. May my responses to others be marked by kindness.

Use me as an agent for bringing healing to those whose hearts hurt. Help me to see opportunities to extend kindness in Jesus' name.

Thank You for the privilege of following Your example. Strengthen me by Your power.

In the name of my kind Savior, I pray. Amen.

The Gift of Compassion

Compassion is the awareness of another's distress and a desire to alleviate it. A spirit of compassion is often born out of one's experience of great need. We can empathize with another's distress when we have experienced distress.

As a youngster in need of a place to live, my mother was taken under the wing of a wonderful teacher, Miss Johansen. I will never forget my mother's stories about her. Miss Johansen was a Christian lady, unmarried, who was beloved and admired in the community. This kind woman took a special interest in my mother, a teenager without a mother and without a place to call home. Miss Johansen befriended my mother and welcomed this lost teenager to her lovely home to live. She was a living lesson to Barbara as she demonstrated the compassion of her Christian faith. Because of the compassion Miss Johansen showed to her, my mother became acutely sensitive to the needs of others.

Miss Johansen also taught my mother about a gracious lifestyle, how to set a table properly, the finer points of etiquette as well as common courtesy, and an appreciation for china, silver, and crystal. This was never about impressing others with material things; this was about respecting others by giving them the best you have to offer. This was about showing compassion by treating others with dignity regardless of their circumstances. In small and large ways, my mother learned to show compassion and to bestow dignity on others by showering them with her best. Everyone deserved compassion, regardless of the person's station in life. This was Miss Johansen's legacy to my mother.

So it is no wonder that out of her circumstances, my mother learned to treat all people with great dignity and to offer compassion whenever the need arose. From working in the tuberculosis ward at Billings Hospital in Chicago as a sixteen-year-old to volunteering at the Victory Mission on skid row in Salinas, California, as the wife of a corporate executive, she constantly showed compassion for others. Even when her body was riddled with cancer and her husband was completely disabled, my mother visited those who were sick, shut in, lonely, or recently bereaved.

Compassion is not only the awareness of another's distress but the desire to alleviate that distress. Compassion compels action. I will never forget the compassion in action of oncologist Dr. David Palchak when my mother was in the final stages of terminal cancer and my father was in the advanced stages of Alzheimer's disease. Extremely sick from chemotherapy, my mother needed after-hours care, so I called Dr. Palchak. He didn't pass us on to the doctor on call. He interrupted his evening and made an immediate house call, arriving as quickly as possible on his street-rocket motorcycle. This was his first of several house calls. When he walked into the living room of their gracious home for the first time and saw my mother and father side by side in hospital beds, I heard him say under his breath, "Oh my." He immediately sympathized with the gravity of the situation and offered the most loving care I have ever seen administered, not only to my mother, his patient, but to my father also.

Upon leaving, Dr. Palchak told me that he was "so very sorry," since we both knew that the care he offered was palliative at best. He offered soul care with his words of sympathy. His recognition of the weight I carried as their daughter was enough to bandage my aching heart and to renew my strength. He expressed compassion through deed and word, providing a living lesson in action.

Have you ever wondered why we suffer if God loves us so much? Why does He allow it? Are we being punished? Much has been written on this subject. Quite simply, suffering is part of the human journey. Jesus suffered, and He was perfect and without sin. Suffering draws us to God in ways that no other experience can. It compels us to rely on God's power, not on our own. It reorders our priorities so that we can live more fully, beyond ourselves. Suffering humbles us, strengthens us, and makes us more sensitive to the needs of others. It plants the seeds of compassion. If we never suffered, we could not identify with the pain of another. Compassion is sympathy in action, born out of suffering.

"You, O Lord, are a compassionate and gracious God, slow to anger, abounding in love and faithfulness" (Ps. 86:15).

"All of you, live in harmony with one another; be sympathetic, love as brothers, be compassionate and humble" (1 Peter 3:8).

"Praise be to the God and Father of our Lord Jesus Christ, the Father of compassion and the God of all comfort, who comforts us in all our troubles, so that we can comfort those in any trouble with the comfort we ourselves have received from God. For just as the sufferings of Christ flow over into our lives, so also through Christ our comfort overflows" (2 Cor. 1:3–5).

"My grace is sufficient for you for my power is made perfect in weakness… When I am weak, then I am strong" (Rom. 12:9–10).

Your life has a purpose. Use your life. Let your difficulties cause you to draw close to God and to trust Him more. In your weakness, He is strong. Out of your troubles, the comfort of compassion can flow from Him through you to others in their time of need. Be that spark to light the darkness!

Compassionate Jesus,

How great is Your love for me that You suffered the ultimate rejection, being put to death for my sin. I cannot comprehend the depth of Your love. You were completely innocent and without fault yet You willingly submitted Yourself to be murdered by the mob to save me. Out of love and compassion for me, You willingly experienced great pain, suffering, and even death to save me.

You have allowed suffering to be part of the human condition for a great purpose, Lord. Forgive me for the self-pity that can overcome my thoughts. Forgive me for the disappointment and disillusionment that I feel toward You when distress occurs.

Help me to accept and to embrace suffering when it comes into my life. Let it draw me to You, Lord. May Your strength replace my weakness. Comfort me in my distress. Focus my attention on those whose sufferings far exceed my own. May I plant seeds of compassion and comfort in the lives of others.

Thank You for Your great love. Help me to remember that I have been created for a special purpose.

Everything You allow is for my good. You have chosen me and I am precious to You. Enable me to be at peace in Your presence, Lord. Let me feel Your love, Jesus, so that I will not focus on temporary difficulties but on what is eternal.

In the name of my compassionate friend, Jesus, I pray. Amen.

The Gift of Wholehearted Trust

On a hot Wednesday night in the fall of 1970, I sat with my family listening to the testimonies of the faithful during a prayer meeting at the Calvary Baptist Church in Quincy, Illinois. I was fourteen years old. I watched as Mary Martens, a middle-aged woman, limped on her badly withered leg to the podium on the platform. The only parts of her story I heard were, "I fully surrendered my life to the Lord," "I got cancer," and "Praise God"—in that order. Her limp and her withered leg resulted from cancer treatment, praise God.

Surely there was more to her story, but those were the three parts that were impressed on my immature understanding. Praise God? I certainly did not want to get cancer and a withered leg, so why would I want to fully surrender my life to the Lord? The seeds of the fear of fully submitting to the Lord's will were sown.

Fast forward to August of 1976. I was in college and engaged to my high school sweetheart. We were planning our wedding for the following summer when we got the news that Bob had a malignant bladder tumor. Thankfully the cancer was in the early stages, and the only treatment required was surgery to remove the tumor with vigilant follow-up for the next five years to be sure the cancer did not return.

We were married one year later as planned. Although I had tried to ignore the possibility of a recurrence, the emotional bonds of marriage and the intense love I felt for my husband as a new bride soon gave way to acute fear. What if the cancer returned? What if we could never have a family, and if we did, what if my children lost their father? What if I became a young widow?

I sought counsel from one of my most well-liked college professors, and although I am sure he said something that should have been reassuring, I came away sensing his concern. After all, he suggested that we wait at least five years before starting our family—good advice but offered for obvious reasons. The suggestion reinforced my anxiety in those first five years when the threat of recurrence loomed.

The fear lasted for many years, and my prayer became a broken record of asking the Lord for complete healing for my husband. But it was prayer without trust, prayer without submission, fear cloaked in prayer. After all, just look at Mary Martens.

Cancer was to be a frequent intruder in the lives of those I love. In 1986, my dear mother-in-law was diagnosed with breast cancer, which later recurred as ovarian cancer. She battled the disease until it finally took her life in 2008. During those same years, my beloved father-in-law died after a one-year battle with colon cancer. And my mother fought her battle with kidney cancer for the last three years of her life and lost. These were devoted Christian people whose great faith sustained them. I watched their struggles up close.

My life too had been one of faith, and God had graciously answered my prayer for complete healing for my husband. But I knew I wasn't completely committed in my faith journey. My faith told me that I could totally trust God, but my heart was fearful. The childish fear of total surrender was never far beneath the surface. What if total submission to the Lord's will meant more cancer or some other tragedy? What if this time it involved me or my sons?

With an empty nest and the loss of my parents and in-laws, my world turned upside down. I felt intense grief and lacked a sense of purpose. I had been a very involved mother, a diligent wife, and a devoted daughter during my parents' final years. Surely the Lord still had use for me. But He seemed silent. I prayed and waited for three years.

Finally one day, I realized that while I was waiting on the Lord, the Lord might be waiting on me! With that realization, I had a chat with the Lord and told Him I was finally "all in." He could do with my life as He pleased. I was His forever. I finally believed, not only in my head but in my heart, that the place of greatest blessing, peace, and purpose would be found in total surrender to God's will, trusting Him completely, letting go of fear once and for all, and thereby living to glorify Him, no matter what. This was a done deal.

About three months later, I was diagnosed with breast cancer in an early stage. Although I was tempted to think, *See, that's what you get for total surrender, just like Mary Martens*, the Lord gave me a sense of peace and trust that did not come naturally to me. Throughout my journey from diagnosis to lumpectomy to seven weeks of daily radiation treatment, God gave me total confidence that my life was in His hands and that I could wholeheartedly trust Him during this trial and any other pothole I might run into on the road of life. My life was no longer my own. Now I knew what Mary Martens meant, and I could say with her, "Praise God." Indeed, praise God.

"The Lord is my strength and my shield; my heart trusts in him, and I am helped. My heart leaps for joy and I will give thanks to him" (Ps. 28:7).

"The Lord's unfailing love surrounds those who trust in Him" (Ps. 32:10).

"Blessed is he who trusts in the Lord" (Prov. 16:20).

"When I am afraid, I will trust in you. In God, whose word I praise, in God I trust; I will not be afraid" (Ps. 56:3–4).

"Trust in the Lord with all your heart and lean not on your own understanding; in all your ways acknowledge him, and he will make your paths straight" (Prov. 3:5–6).

"May the God of hope fill you with all joy and peace as you trust in him, so that you may overflow with hope by the power of the Holy Spirit" (Rom. 15:13).

"Trust in the Lord forever, for the Lord, the Lord, is the Rock eternal" (Isa. 26:4).

So I invite you to place your trust wholeheartedly in the only one who is completely worthy of your trust, the Lord Jesus Christ. In all circumstances, trust Him, and experience the peace that passes all understanding. Incredible blessing comes out of our brokenness, for it draws us to Him and releases His power to work in our lives. Leave your burdens at the foot of the cross. The Lord gave His life to free you. Trust Him and Him alone—always and no matter what. His will for you is perfect, and His faithfulness is never-ending. His blessings are indeed abundant.

You are trustworthy, Lord, and Your patience is unfailing. Your faithfulness is never-ending.

You are compassionate and merciful. I love You and bow in humility before You.

Forgive me for my inclination to control my circumstances and for my failure to trust You. Remove all traces of fear from my heart and mind.

Thank You for Your patience, Lord, and for not giving up on me.

You are in control of every detail of my life, and Your resources are abundant. Your power is limitless. You know the needs of my life and the desires of my heart.

Help me to live in the light of Your great love for me. Help me to cast all my burdens on You and to enjoy the peace that comes from trusting You completely. For You are worthy beyond my comprehension.

To center my trust in You is the greatest blessing and joy. Fill my heart with total trust in You and in You alone.

Be my rock, Lord, and when the waves of life crash, may I set my anchor on You.

In the name of my trustworthy Savior, I pray. Amen.

The Gift of Gratitude

During the final eleven months of my mother's life, I had the privilege of attending a cancer support group with her twice each month. It was a profound experience, a bright light on an otherwise dark path. We were surrounded by other cancer warriors and survivors, people who knew deeply the value of each day. They shared difficulties, offered encouragement, reported the latest medical information, and above all, told jokes and enjoyed laughter. How could these beautiful people, whose lives in most cases would soon be ended by their dreadful disease, find joy and laugh at their circumstances?

I soon learned their secret. They had discovered the gift of gratitude. Talk to people who know the number of their days and you will find a deep awareness and appreciation for the value in each and every moment. Suddenly, the world has become a place of greater beauty than they had realized when they were healthier. Colors are more brilliant. The songs of birds are sweeter. Music is lovelier. Simple pleasures take on major significance. Relationships are of the highest value. Giving and receiving love are life's greatest treasures. Gratitude infuses their outlook on life with positivity and hope. They find something in each day for which to be grateful. The present is a present! And herein lies their joy—living to the fullest while alive! The secret is gratitude.

Gratitude was the source of my mother's greatest joy. She was grateful that her completely incapacitated husband still shared life with her. She was grateful for their many blessings. She was grateful for the excellent care she and her beloved received. She was grateful for the loving concern of friends and family. She was grateful for her daily bread. While medical expenses were high, she was grateful for financial provision.

My mother greeted each day with the joy of the Lord in her heart, knowing that His mercies were new every morning. Gratitude lifted her spirits. Gratitude assured her that whatever she had, no matter how little or how much, it was enough to face anything the day had in store for her. My mother's attitude of gratitude opened her eyes to the many gifts that remained in her life even while it was ebbing away.

Gratitude is the gift that keeps on giving. It is a powerful, transforming force. It changes the landscape of our lives, infusing light and hope in the dark places. Thankfulness, despite and even because of our circumstances, gifts us with renewal, spiritual healing, joy, and wholeness. It reconnects us with what is most important in life, those simple, everyday miracles that we often overlook.

"In everything, give thanks" (1 Thess. 5:18).

"Be thankful" (Col. 3:15).

"Give thanks to the Lord, for He is good; his love endures forever" (Ps. 107:1).

"Thanks be to God! He gives of victory through our Lord Jesus Christ" (1 Cor. 15:57).

"Because of the Lord's great love we are not consumed, for his compassions never fail. They are new every morning" (Lam. 3:23).

When we cultivate an attitude of gratitude, we find that every day is a gift to be cherished. And gratitude is most powerful in the midst of our greatest difficulties. It broadens our perspective, helping us to see the larger picture of our lives and to refocus on the good things. So give thanks, not only for the obvious but for the not-so-obvious. You will be amazed to discover the wholeness of your life, no matter how broken it may otherwise seem.

Merciful Father,

Your mercies are indeed new every morning.

You provide for my every need. Every day is full of Your blessings in my life.

Great is Your faithfulness. I thank You, Lord, for that.

I thank You for Your steadfast love.

I thank You for Your goodness in all circumstances.

I thank You for Your grace.

I thank You for Your mercy.

I thank You for Your compassion.

I thank You for Your forgiveness.

I thank You for the beauty that surrounds me.

I thank You for meeting my every need.

I thank You for being all that I need.

May my attitude be characterized by gratitude, may my thoughts be infused with gratitude, and may my life be one that exudes gratitude daily.

Thank You, Lord. Amen.

The Gift of Grace

Grace is unmerited favor. Have you ever received a gift from someone that took you completely by surprise? A gift that you did nothing to deserve or to earn? A gift given purely from the love and generosity spilling out of the heart of another? How did that make you feel? Were you overwhelmed by a sense of gratitude and bewildered at the goodness of the giver, having done nothing to receive such a gift? Surely, you have had such an experience. It didn't necessarily involve a grand gift. It could have been the humblest of gestures, a simple, thoughtful act of kindness toward you.

During the seven weeks of my daily radiation treatment, I received a gift of grace from my brother that I will never forget. He called me daily to count down the days with me, reminding me that with the passing of each one I was closer to the end of treatment. He never missed a call. He took time out of his busy life to offer encouragement every day. He walked through the process from a distance with me. Did he do this as payback for something? No. This was a simple gift of grace from the goodness of his heart.

My dear brother made another such gesture this past summer. One of my sons was planning for his wedding. He and his fiancée were on a tight budget and saving all they could for their wedding celebration. There were priorities to be met and sacrifices to be made to accommodate a guest list that showed no partiality. The list included people making up the fabric of their lives: family, and friends including college and seminary professors, a onetime homeless person, and many folks in between.

My brother became aware of the couple's budget concerns. From his big and generous heart, he felt prompted to offer a gift to cover the cost of one of the high-ticket items on their priority list of wedding costs. Taking great delight in this prompting, he crafted a grand surprise. He sent a letter to his nephew, my son, with instructions to take his fiancée out for a special dinner at a place they could not otherwise afford. Not only was the meal paid for, but enclosed with the letter was a message to be opened by candlelight as they shared a bottle of wine. The message told them of a significant gift toward one of their major wedding expenses.

To say that my son and his fiancée were overwhelmed is an understatement. I too was dumbfounded. Did they do anything to deserve this gift? Did they do anything to earn it? Was it owed to them? No. It came to them simply out of the goodness and generosity of my brother's heart in response to a perceived need and to the prompting of the Holy Spirit. It was a gift of grace—free and unearned with no strings attached and with the expectation of nothing in return.

The motivation for such gifts comes from gratitude for the grace we have received from God, the giver of all good and perfect gifts. My brother took great delight in giving this gift of grace. Whether we have much or little, we all have gifts of grace to give others. Whether it be a kind word, an empathetic ear, a shared tear, or a thoughtful gesture, we can give the gift of grace, something unearned and undeserved for the benefit of someone else. It doesn't have to cost a cent. Gifts of grace are given with no expectation of something in return. We need only be aware of and grateful for God's goodness to us and alert to the needs of others. No matter our circumstances, we can always find someone whose need is greater than our own.

To become a grace-gifter, you must have a sensitivity to the needs and circumstances of others. For some, this sensitivity comes naturally. For others, it must be cultivated. Practice putting others first. Ask yourself what you can do to make a difference in the life of another when the opportunity presents itself. Then act joyfully! The joy will be returned to you multiplied.

God has lavished His abundant grace upon us because of His great love for us. All we have to do is to accept His free gifts. There are many for the taking, the greatest of all being the gift of eternal life through Jesus Christ, His Son.

> Because of His great love for us, God, who is rich in mercy, made us alive with Christ even when we were dead in transgressions—it is by grace you have been saved. And God raised us up with Christ and seated us with him in the heavenly realms in Christ Jesus, in order that in the coming ages he might show the incomparable riches of his grace, expressed in his kindness to us in Christ Jesus. For it is by grace you have been saved, through faith—and this not from yourselves; it is the gift of God... For we are God's workmanship, created in Christ Jesus to

do good works, which God prepared in advance for us to do. (Eph. 2:4–8, 10)

Do you think you are worthless? Do you think you have nothing to give, nothing to offer? Do you think that you can't make a difference? Open the gift of grace. Accept God's love for you, and resolve to believe that you have great worth to Him—so much so that He gave His Son to die for your sins so that you can live an abundant, grace-filled life now and spend eternity with Him. That is the greatest gift of all. You can do nothing to earn it. Simply receive it freely, and give grace freely every chance you get! Therein lies great self-worth.

Gracious and loving Father,

Your grace is abundant in every way. You lavish it upon us for the taking. And Your grace is more than we could ever ask or need.

I thank You and praise You for Your generous gifts of grace in my life.

Increase my awareness of opportunities to extend these gifts to others. Empower me by the knowledge of Your great grace in my life.

May Your grace motivate me to show grace to others in whatever ways You lead. May my life reflect the sweet beauty of Your grace and point others to You.

In Your gracious name, I pray. Amen.

The Gift of Friendship

Friendship is the topic of many volumes, for in our friendships we discover one of life's greatest blessings. We are born into a family, but we choose our friends. True friends stick with us through thick and thin. They accept us as we are, give without expecting anything in return, and help us to believe in ourselves when we have ceased to believe. It has been said that friends are the blossoms in the garden of life. God takes care of us through our friends. Not only do we nurture them, but they nurture us.

I have always had many casual friends but only a handful of close ones. Tracie is my longest-standing friend. We have been friends since second grade, more than fifty-one years! As my best friend from childhood, she has unique insight into my life. She knew my siblings. She knew my parents. As a child, she was embraced as part of my extended family. We shared secrets. We enjoyed slumber parties. We took part in extracurricular activities together. Our birthdays are only three days apart. We rode bikes to each other's houses. We played together. We walked to school together. We shared the ups and downs of childhood.

Tracie and I met when we were the new kids in the second grade at Monterey Park School. Her family had moved to Salinas about the same time as mine. She must have known of the meanness of two of our classmates toward me, but she never once was unkind to me. She remained a loyal friend all during those elementary years. Her loyalty gave me the confidence I needed to feel accepted.

Jane and I met on our first day of freshman orientation at Wheaton College in the fall of 1974. We have been the best of friends ever since, for more than forty years now. Our hearts connected instantly with an easy and natural geniality. We experienced college life together, and she was my roommate until marriage. I have never known a more thoughtful person. Her acts of care and consideration for me taught me how to be a friend. Jane is steadfast, always offering encouragement and showing loving concern by her actions and always ready to enjoy an easy laugh. She is not only my friend but my sister—my sister by another mother.

We have shared the pursuits of careers, the joys and the challenges of raising a family, the sorrows of losing our parents, and the fun of empty nest adventures. Jane has shown love for my family, traveling great distances to participate in our significant life events. She has been there for me in the good times and the bad. She accepts me no matter what. Jane nurtures my spirit. She is a friend in the truest sense.

I could mention other friends who have blessed my life, but instead I would like to fast forward to the greatest gift of friendship I have received in recent years. I have a dear sister-in-law named Jan. I knew of her when I was a high school student and never dreamed then that she would many years later become my sister through marriage to my brother. And a true sister she is. Jan is the most extraordinary of friends. She has shown unconditional, selfless love in countless ways. Jan is an ICU post-surgical cardiac nurse who has saved countless lives, and she has tears with families at the bedsides of patients whose lives cannot be saved.

Jan demonstrated tireless care, unconditional love, and support at the bedsides of my dying parents. She used every medical trick in the book to provide palliative care and to improve the quality of life of her dying mother-in-law and father-in law, my mom and dad. Her life exudes compassion and an understanding of human frailties that become apparent under the most difficult of circumstances.

She was there for me equally, taking time off from work to give me respite, consulting over confounding medical challenges, commiserating with me over the most loving of all burdens, that of caring for dying parents, and supporting me when the emotional stresses exceeded my ability to cope. In short, she gave me strength to complete a God-given task, to go the distance, and to finish strong. She is a master at matters of the heart, literally and figuratively!

True friends etch their names on our hearts. They share life's joys and life's pains. In the tough times, true friends practice uncommon compassion and radical mercy. In those tough times the value of their cherished role in our lives becomes tangible as their selflessness strengthens us in the broken places. God reaches down and takes care of us through them.

"He who refreshes others will himself be refreshed" (Prov. 11:25).

"If one falls down, his friend can help him up" (Eccles. 4:10).

"A friend loves at all times" (Prov. 17:17).

"A man of many companions may come to ruin, but there is a friend who sticks closer than a brother" (Prov. 18:24).

"For great is his love toward us, and the faithfulness of the Lord endures forever" (Ps. 117:2).

"The Lord is near to all who call upon him" (Ps. 145:18).

"Greater love has no one than this, that one lay down his life for his friends" (John 15:13).

My mother's favorite hymn during her final years was an old tune called "My God and I," written in the 1930s by I. B. Sergei. The sweet words tell of the friendship between a traveler on life's journey and God, a friendship that would "go unendingly." Mom learned to play this lovely tune on the piano and would sing its beautiful words for my father to enjoy as the shades were closing on his life. I too played it for them repeatedly on the piano during the last months of their lives. My dying mother sang along with strength and confidence in her frail voice. She found great comfort despite her terminal condition because she knew her friend was walking with her to her eternal home.

The friends who have blessed my life remind me of the faithfulness of Jesus toward His friends. Jesus called His followers "friends." He accepts us without condition. He binds up our wounds. He gives guidance. He extends grace and compassion. He loves us with an unshakable love. He is patient with us. He cares about every detail of our lives. He walks with us to our eternal home.

Dearest Friend,

Thank You for the life-sustaining gift of friendship.

It is only because of Your great love for us that we can love one another.

I am grateful for the experience of Your grace through human friendships.

Show me how I can encourage someone else today. Give me eyes to see and ears to hear the needs of those around me. Help me to make time for meaningful relationships.

May I be to my friends all that they are to me. Let my life reflect my friendship with You, and may I be that friend who sticks closer than a sister. Amen.

The Gift of Life through Death

It was Monday, October 6, 2008. Mom had not awakened since Saturday. She had slipped into a coma. A heat wave had arrived on the otherwise mild central coast of California. Sharon, our faithful caregiver, and I kept the house as cool as possible, but still it was uncomfortably warm. I soothed my mother's body with damp washcloths and moistened her lips with lip balm. We changed her position in bed frequently to avoid the formation of bedsores on her bony and wasted frame. I slept at her bedside at night. There were no more visitors now. These were sacred days because God was near. I played her favorite tune, "My God and I," for her on the piano. I whispered in her ear that famous and beloved psalm of David, the twenty-third.

The Lord is my shepherd, I shall lack nothing. He makes me lie down in green pastures, he leads me beside quiet waters, he restores my soul. He guides me in the paths of righteousness for his name's sake. Even though I walk through the valley of the shadow of death, I will fear no evil, for you are with me; your rod and your staff, they comfort me. You prepare a table before me in the presence of my enemies. You anoint my head with oil; my cup overflows. Surely goodness and love will follow me all the days of my life, and I will dwell in the house of the Lord forever.

This routine continued for three more days. Mom was the focus of our attention. Dad was holding his own in his incapacitated state. When I said good-bye to Sharon as she left on Thursday, we both sensed that she would return to care only for my father the following day.

Bob and I kept the nightly vigil at my parents' bedsides. Dad had drifted off to sleep. I was on a twin bed next to my mother's bed so that I could monitor her condition and keep her cool. Hospice partners had described the signs that would indicate that life was coming to an end. I kept my hand on her wrist and noticed her heartbeat becoming irregular. At 10:58 p.m., I heard the death rattle, that mysterious clicking at the back of a dying person's throat as the end nears. "Fly to Jesus, Mom. Fly to Jesus," I whispered as I choked back the tears. I felt her heartbeat; it was her last, and God came. It was 11:00 p.m. The moment was sacred. I called my dear brother and reported Mom's home-going. "Mom is in heaven now," I said.

Two young men arrived about an hour later, dressed in black suits and with solemn expressions on their faces. They asked me to remove Mom's wedding ring from her finger, and also Dad's wedding ring, which she had worn on a chain around her neck ever since he had become disabled. Doing it broke my heart. I asked them to treat her kindly because she was a beautiful woman. I kissed my mother and told her one last time that I loved her. The men left the room to get the gurney. The room was dark, the only light coming from the adjacent entry hall.

I moved to my dear dad's bedside so as not to face what was about to happen. Dad had awakened, but I will never know if he realized what had just taken place. I think he knew somehow. I heard the legs of the gurney snap into place, and I sobbed uncontrollably at the rails of my father's bed. I heard the rustling of the sheets, the whispers of my kind husband and the young men, the squeaking of the gurney wheels. The front door shut. Mom was gone, loaded into the back of a van. Gone forever, or so it seemed.

The next few days were a blur of activity. Dad's condition took a turn for the worse. He could no longer swallow. His breathing seemed congested. Hospice nurses told us that he had a urinary tract infection. It was the first time his condition had seriously deteriorated in the five years that he had been bedridden and completely disabled. The familiar signs of life's end were becoming evident.

By Wednesday night, October 15, God was coming for Dad. Following dinner, brought to the house by a friend, other family members had gone upstairs to watch Barack Obama in one of his final debates prior to the November 2008 election. I sat at Dad's bedside and repeated the routine I had used for Mom, whispering Psalm 23 in his ear. He opened his beautiful blue eyes briefly one last time. These were my last moments with my daddy. I noticed that his neck no longer supported his head. I knew this would be his last evening with us.

My brother insisted that I go home and let him stay the night with Dad. He sensed that I could not endure another departure.

He assured me he would stay at Dad's bedside. He dutifully called me to share the news a few hours later. To this day, I am grateful for the strength and sensitivity of my brother. Dad was now in heaven too.

Three days later, we buried my mother and father in flag-draped caskets with military honors as we celebrated their lives and their faith in a beautiful joint graveside service. And one last time, we sang "My God and I."

A gift of life through death? Now if that is not counterintuitive, I don't know what is! But there is profound truth in the words "life through death." I am writing of eternal life, which starts in the here and now and continues through death.

Eternal life starts when we make a deliberate choice to "die" daily to self-interest. Only by putting the needs of others before our own and living a life of service to others do we find life in the present—abundant life now! By dying to self, caring about others, and being other-oriented, we find life. Giving up our self-interest for the service of others brings us the life we seek.

Because I am a Christian, I believe that the Bible is God's revealed truth. And I believe the well-known passage, John 3:16, which states, "For God so loved the world that he gave his one and only Son, that whoever believes in him shall not perish but have eternal life." The physical death of our bodies is rebirth. Physical death ushers the believer into eternal life beyond the present.

The physical death of a loved one tests our faith. It is where the rubber meets the road. And my faith was certainly tested by the deep grief I experienced when I lost my parents in one week and my dear mother-in-law, all in less than a month. Their deaths put me into a tailspin. While I believed in my head that they were indeed in a better place, healed, and with the Lord Jesus Christ, my heart and my emotions were shattered. Death seemed so final. They were gone. And gone through death is gone forever, never to be again in this life. This was unfathomable to me. I could not wrap my heart around this new reality.

My focus was on their bodies in the ground. When it was cold outside, I feared they were cold. When it rained, I feared they would be wet. And I could not do anything about it. I couldn't visit their graves because I could not bear to think that my loved ones were in the ground. I went out of my way if necessary to avoid driving by the cemetery.

My dear husband's response to the grief we shared was entirely different. While he ached for our losses, he found solace in the knowledge that we would one day be reunited in heaven with our loved ones. Yes, their bodies are in the ground, but they are not there! His unshakable knowledge and hope were rooted in the resurrection of Jesus Christ. After all, Jesus Christ conquered death through His resurrection, and He promises the same victory and eternal life to those who believe. My husband believed with his head and his heart.

I struggled for many, many months. I would pray for comfort, but God seemed deafeningly silent. Then one night while asleep, I saw my mother and father dancing in a beautiful place, with a joy on their faces and a glow about them that I had never seen before.

When I awoke the next morning, I was perplexed until I realized that God in His grace had given me a glimpse into heaven through that dream. I shared the dream with my husband, who without hesitation responded that God had given me a gift, a confirmation that while our earthly bodies die, those who believe indeed have eternal life. My struggle was over. My heart was healed. I can now go by the cemetery and know that while their earthly bodies are in the ground, my loved ones have been reborn to eternal life. They have risen to new life. And we will one day be reunited for eternity.

We die to self in this life to experience the fullness of life on earth, and we gain eternal life through physical death when the Lord calls us to our eternal home. This is the gift of life through death. This is the reality of faith, faith in God through Jesus Christ, and in Him alone.

"May the God of hope fill you with all joy and peace as you trust in him, so that you may overflow with the hope by the power of the Holy Spirit" (Rom. 15:13).

"For the Lord is good and his love endures forever; his faithfulness continues through all generations" (Ps. 100:5).

"If we died with him, we shall also live with him" (2 Tim. 2:11).

"I am the resurrection and the life. He who believes in me will live, even though he dies" (John 11:25).

"Do not let your hearts be troubled. Trust in God; trust also in me. In my Father's house are many rooms... I am going to prepare a place for you... I will come back and take you to be with me that you also may be where I am" (John 14:1–3).

There is no hope apart from faith and trust in Jesus Christ. Hope anchors our feet firmly on earth, while our hearts and minds see a life that is far bigger. Christian hope transcends the circumstances of this life. And hope in Christ alone establishes peace in our hearts as we stand in otherwise hopeless places. We can indeed trust in His resurrection power. He is worthy!

Victorious Lord,

Though this life can be stained with tears and the journey marked with pain, my eternal hope is in You and in Your resurrection power alone. And in that truth we find great joy!

Thank You for the cross. Thank You for Your absolute victory over death.

Thank You for the promise of eternal life for those who believe and put their trust in You.

Thank You that through You, we will one day be reunited with our loved ones who trusted You as their Savior and have gone before us.

I commit my spirit and my life to You.

Strengthen my faith, and anchor me in Your love. Teach me to walk in Your ways.

May my life on earth bring glory to You and lead others to faith in You. Amen.

The Gift of Giving

I was cruising along on my bike this morning, and as I rode, I asked the Lord the question I ask Him every day. What act of kindness can I do for someone else today? Soon my mind wandered on to more pressing matters of the day, especially how I was going to make it up the steep hill ahead!

As I rode past the freeway off-ramp on the frontage road, there sat a man on the curb with his dog. He held up a tattered cardboard sign that read, "Me and dog—hungry—need food." He had long, bedraggled hair, a scraggly beard, dirty, ragged clothes, tanned, leather skin, and a blistered bald spot and scabs on his head from exposure to the elements. I smiled and nodded to him as I cruised by. I got only a few yards farther down the road when I realized I had the answer to my earlier prayer.

I don't often have money with me on my rides, but this morning, I heeded my husband's suggestion that I take some along, just in case. The Lord brought to mind the money in my back pocket and prompted me to turn around and give it away. I didn't need to know the man's story or if he was "legit." I would just do it.

As I approached him, I told him I had been asking the Lord how I might help someone else this day and was directed back to him. I dug around in my back pocket and handed the man a ten-dollar bill. It wasn't much, but it was what I had to give. I could only trust that it would be put to good use.

The man's response was remarkable. He told me of his troubles but not in a way to evoke sympathy. We talked for at least thirty minutes as cars passed by. Some drivers looked on with concern, while others ignored us.

He told me of his homelessness. He had had a choice to make—to give up his place to live or to give up his dog, and he chose to keep his dog. His thin body had been wrecked by years of self-destructive behavior. He had severe Crohn's disease, and as he put it, "My guts are running out of my body." He had been a heroin addict for many years, but three years ago, God had delivered him. He proceeded to give the most beautiful witness to God's grace I have ever heard. He told me of God's mercy. He told me of God's grace. He told me of God's compassion. He told me of God's provision. He told me that God provides enough for each day and that it is always enough.

His words were peppered with Scripture, the true bread of his life. He knew his Bible well. He sang lyrics from worship music. He told me that while he realized the world didn't value a person such as himself, he knew he had incredible worth as a child of God. He quoted the words of Jesus in Luke 12:15: "A man's life does not consist in the abundance of his possessions." And while he didn't know how much time he had left on this earth, he looked forward to eternal life in heaven through the sacrifice of his Savior, Jesus Christ. He was certain that God was all he needed for this day and forever.

As I listened, I felt at times like I was talking to Jesus Himself. This homeless man's words were sincere and powerful. He humbled me. I thought I was doing something for someone else, but it was I who received the far greater blessing. When I was about to leave, I asked the man his name. I said, "God bless you, Brian," to which he replied, "Oh, He does. He does."

As I rode off, my heart was overwhelmed by the encounter. I felt as if God had showed up in my life and taken me completely by surprise through the words of a homeless man with his dog on the side of the road. Not only did I experience the joy of giving, but I received a blessing in return many times over.

As my bike route took me by the cemetery, I thought of my mother and father buried there and remembered my mother's story of being without a place to call home. I recalled her countless acts of giving to those in need as a result of her hardships as a teenager. I whispered a prayer of thanks for my mother and father, who taught me by the example of their lives. And truly, as Jesus taught, "It is more blessed to give than to receive." The blessing is in the giving because it takes us outside of ourselves, and it is precisely there that we encounter God.

"Give us this day our daily bread" (Matt. 6:11).

"In everything, do to others what you would have them do to you" (Matt. 7:12).

"Freely you have received. Freely give" (Matt. 10:8).

"Give and it will be given to you. A good measure, pressed down, shaken together and running over, will be poured into your lap" (Luke 6:38).

"I give them eternal life, and they shall never perish; no one can snatch them out of my hand" (John 10:28).

"Peace I leave with you; my peace I give you" (John 14:27).

The Scripture verses above are the recorded words of Jesus. The act of giving was vitally important to Jesus—so much so that He gave His very life for us. And He calls us to do the same by giving from our lives to bless others in His name and for His sake—all for His eternal purpose and glory.

Generous Lord,

You are my Father in heaven. You gave Your life for me, and I thank You with my whole heart.

I bow before You and acknowledge my total dependence on You.

Thank You for providing for my every need. Thank You for calling me Your own.

I am grateful for the reminder of Your faithfulness through those in greatest need. They testify in a concrete way to Your faithfulness through their total reliance on Your provision of their daily bread.

May I pay attention to the needs around me, and may I be alert to opportunities to use the resources You have given to me to bless others in Your name.

In the name of Jesus, I pray. Amen.

Marked by His Presence

As I look back over the reflections shared here, I wonder how to land this plane. Our lives tell a story, and mine is still unfolding, as is yours if you are reading this narrative! No one's life is perfect, no matter how charmed it appears from the outside. God gives us more than enough to meet each need. He has already sought us out; His love for us doesn't demand; it just gives and gives and gives. It cannot be exhausted. His goodness and mercy are everlasting. We can trust Him. Nothing can separate us from His love—nothing.

"For I am convinced that neither death nor life, neither angels nor demons, neither the present nor the future, nor any powers, neither height nor depth, nor anything else in all creation, will be able to separate us from the love of God that is in Christ Jesus our Lord" (Rom. 8:38–39).

Life's passages are bittersweet. It has been fifty-two years since my encounter with extreme unkindness. It has been thirty-eight years since my husband's bladder cancer diagnosis. It has been eight and ten years since we launched our beloved sons. It has been six years since we buried our parents. It has been two years since my breast cancer diagnosis and treatment. I am still uncertain of my racial heritage. Through all of these events, I have discovered that the most profound gift is the experience of God's goodness. His goodness comes to us many times through unexpected gifts in unexpected places. Look deeper and you will find them.

And so, as did my mother and my grandfather, I can sing with certainty the words of the old, beloved hymn, "In the Garden." Indeed, "He walks with me, and He talks with me, and He tells me I am His own" in the garden of life with all of its thorns and beauty. He is the gardener, pruning my imperfect life for my good and for His glory. I am His and He is mine.

Look deeper and love the people in your life like there is no tomorrow. Look deeper and find the silver lining in every circumstance. Look deeper and look forward. Look deeper and find unexpected gifts. Look deeper and find God.

May your life be marked by His presence, and may you be clothed in His grace.

Look deeper.

CPSIA information can be obtained
at www.ICGtesting.com
Printed in the USA
FSOW01n2213270716
23176FS